I LOVE to PRAY

A Devotional to Connect You with Jesus

By Kathleen Trock

PRAYERSHOP PUBLISHING

Terre Haute, Indiana

PrayerShop Publishing is the publishing arm of Harvest Prayer Ministries and the Church Prayer Leaders Network. Harvest Prayer Ministries exists to transform lives through teaching prayer.

Its online prayer store, www.prayershop.org, has more than 600 prayer resources available for purchase.

Based upon *Love to Pray* by Alvin VanderGriend

ISBN: 978-1-935012-13-9

1 2 3 4 5 6 7 | 2015 2014 2013 2012 2011 2010 2009

Contents

Introduction

Did you know that Jesus (who is God) hears the prayers of children? The first prayer God answered in the Bible was the prayer of a young boy who was crying. God sent an angel to the boy's mother to tell her that He had heard her child crying and that He would help him (Genesis 21:14–20).

This book will teach you about different kinds of prayer. As you pray during the next forty days you will get to know Jesus better, like getting to know a best friend.

How to use your *I Love to Pray* devotional:

1. Choose a special place and time to read *I Love to Pray* and to talk with Jesus.
2. Take your time with each devotional. Don't rush! God will speak to you through His Word.
3. Read the Bible verse and think about what it means.
4. Ask the Holy Spirit to teach you how to pray and then pray.
5. Show your parents what you have done each day. Talk to them about what you have learned and ask questions about what you don't understand.
6. Share what you have learned with your friends, neighbors, and classmates.
7. Ask Jesus to help you learn to love praying.

WHAT'S THE GOOD OF PRAYER?

"What's the good of prayer anyhow?" asked Tommy.

"What's the good of spending time with your best friend?" his teacher asked. Shrugging his shoulders, Tommy answered, "Everyone knows that you spend time with your best friend because you like to be with him. Even when you're not with him, you still think about him and look forward to seeing him again. I like being with my best friend. It's fun! One time my best friend gave me his last cookie because he could tell that I wanted it."

Tommy's teacher replied, "Prayer is not just talking to God. It's also spending time with God as you would with your best friend, and learning the ways God speaks to you. As you learn what He wants for you and for others, you can ask Him for those things. Prayer is also thanking Him for all the good things He has done and for the special ways that He takes care of you and those you love. It is also confessing the wrong things you have done and hearing Him tell you that you are forgiven. You can tell God how great He is and ask Him for help when you need it. Prayer will help you get to know God, like your best friend. Through prayer you become part of God's story."

"Umm, I never thought about it like that before," said Tommy.

In Week One you will discover the importance of prayer.

Week one, DAY 1

FRIENDSHIP WITH GOD

I have called you friends. I have told you everything I learned from my Father. —JOHN 15:15B

Do you have a best friend?

_____

What do you enjoy doing with your best friend, or what would you enjoy doing with a best friend?

_____

_____

_____

José could not wait for school to be over. He and his best friend, Alex, were going to the baseball field. During the long walk to the field, José was looking forward to telling Alex about Nathan, the new boy who had moved into the neighborhood. Nathan was a great ballplayer. José smiled as he thought about how easy it was to talk to Alex and all the good times that they had together.

It's good to have a best friend. You can have fun together and share your dreams and ideas and secrets. Just as José called Alex his friend, Jesus called the people who liked to be with Him, "His

9

friends." Jesus is the friend who died for you and forgives all of your sins. He invites you to be His friend too. Spending time with Jesus, sharing your thoughts, feelings, and questions with Him and listening for His answers is called "prayer." Prayer is the talking that goes on between you and God.*

Just as you make plans to be with your friends, it is important to plan time to be with God.

Where and when will you plan to spend time with Jesus?

_____

_____

_____

What are some of the things that you want to thank Jesus for today?

_____

_____

_____

What do you want to talk to Him about?

_____

_____

_____

Spend some time today, telling Jesus how much you love Him and listen for how He might speak to you. Write down what He says.

_____

_____

_____

_____

Today's prayer:

_____

_____

_____

_____

_____

_____

*Story taken from *God Speaks*, a Pebbles and Stones curriculum, copyright 2007.

TEACH US TO PRAY

In the same way, the Holy Spirit helps us when we are weak. We don't know what we should pray for. But the Spirit himself prays for us. He prays with groans too deep for words. God, who looks into our hearts, knows the mind of the Spirit. And the Spirit prays for God's people just as God wants him to pray. —ROMANS 8:26-27

Have you ever been in a situation where you didn't know what to do? What was the situation and what did you do?

_____

_____

_____

_____

Did you ask anyone to help you? _____ What did they do?

_____

_____

_____

_____

Sometimes we may see something and think we know how to pray about it. The truth is that we don't know what we should pray for, but the Holy Spirit will pray with us and show us what to pray. A few years ago, I was in Ethiopia. A pastor asked me if I would go to the house of a woman whose children had been kidnapped and pray for her. I remember praying, "God, I don't know what to pray or how to pray for her. Would you please give me your prayer for her?" After I had prayed, I saw a picture in my thoughts of a woman writing something on a piece of paper and putting it into the hand of one of three children. I saw the children gathered around a small soiled and torn paper. They were reading it and smiling at each other. When I shared this with the woman, she cried and said that she had written Psalm 23 on a paper and put it into the hand of one of her children the night before they were taken away, and now she felt that her children were safe.*

It has been a few years since I prayed with this woman in Ethiopia. God not only took away her sadness that day, but He also returned her children safely. Today, she and her children are living in Canada.

You don't have to worry about what you should pray, or how you should pray. Prayer is God's idea; He will show you what and who to pray for through the Holy Spirit. How does He do this? You may be walking and suddenly think about somebody. That thought might be the Holy Spirit reminding you to pray for that person. Remember, prayer is talking with God and listening for Him too.

Before you start to pray today, ask God to show you what to pray and who to pray for. Write that down here:

_____

_____

_____

Today's prayer:

_____

_____

_____

_____

_____

_____

_____

*Story taken from *God Speaks*, a Pebbles and Stones curriculum, copyright 2007.

CELEBRATING GOD THROUGH PRAYER

I will thank the Lord at all times. My lips will always praise him.

I will honor the Lord. Let those who are hurting hear and be joyful.

Join me in giving glory to the Lord. Let us honor him together. —PSALM 34:1-3

How do you show someone that you think he or she is the "best"?

_____

_____

_____

What do you say to him or her?

_____

_____

_____

Moriah blew up purple balloons and tied them to her mother's favorite chair. Purple was her mother's favorite color. She placed her mother's slippers by the chair and put her mother's devotional on the end table. Her mother had been in the hospital and was well enough now to come home. Just then the door opened, and her mother walked into the room. Moriah ran toward her with open arms shouting, "I love you, Mom! I missed you."

When you love someone as Moriah loved her mom, you tell them that you love them, thank them for the things that they do for you, and honor them by doing things for them that you know they will like. Psalm 34 shows us how David praised, thanked, and honored God, and invited others to do the same.

What can you praise God for?

_____

_____

_____

What can you thank God for?

_____

_____

_____

What can you do to honor God today?

_____

_____

_____

Use your answers from above and turn them into prayers.

For example, you may have written, "for all the beauty that I see around me." You can pray, "God, I praise You for all the beautiful things that I see, like birds and flowers."

You may have written, "for my friends." You can pray, "God, I thank You for giving me friends to play with."

We honor God by doing the things He wants us to do. Your prayer can be like this, "God, please help me to obey my mom today." Take a few moments to be in awe of the God Who made you and enjoys being with you.

Today's prayer:

_____

_____

_____

_____

_____

_____

GOD WORKS THROUGH OUR PRAYERS

As long as Moses held his hands up, the Israelites were winning. But every time he lowered his hands, the Amalekites began to win. —EXODUS 17:11

Have you ever started something and then quit? What was it?

_____

_____

_____

All of us, at one time or another have started out to do something and then decided not to finish it. Perhaps we decided it wasn't as much fun as we thought it would be, or it was too hard, or we got tired. A few thousand years ago, Moses, a leader of Israel, started to pray over a battle that his men were fighting. He held his hands up toward God. As long as he held up his hands, his men would win. As the battle continued, Moses' arms became tired, and he lowered them. Then the Amalekites (God's enemies) began to win. So, Moses would lift his hands again to pray, and the Israelites began to win again. Whenever Moses' hands were lifted up, the Israelites would be winning, but when he lowered them, the Amalekites would begin to win. At one point Moses was too tired to hold his hands up any longer. His friends, Aaron and Hur, helped to hold up Moses' hands and the Israelites won the battle. Of course, God is all-powerful and all-wise. He can work without us, but He chooses to work through our prayers. Moses and his men learned something important about prayer. They learned to keep praying, to not give up, and they learned the importance of having others pray with them. They also learned that God wanted them to know the battle would be won through prayer.

Take a few moments to read and think about this story found in the book of Exodus (chapter 17). What did you learn from the story?

_____

_____

_____

_____

What have you been praying about for a long time?

_____

_____

_____

Moses needed Aaron and Hur to help him. Who can you ask to pray with you?

_____

Today's prayer:

_____

_____

_____

_____

_____

_____

_____

YOU'RE WELCOME TO THE THRONE

So let us boldly approach the throne of grace. Then we will receive mercy. We will find grace to help us when we need it. —HEBREWS 4:16

If you were asked to come to the throne of the greatest king who ever lived, how would you feel? Would you wonder why you were invited? Would you go? What would you say?

_____

_____

_____

_____

God, the King of kings, invites you to come near to His throne of grace, a throne where you are always welcomed and loved. He invites you to His throne to show you His kindness and to give you mercy. Mercy means that God does *not* give us what we deserve. We all deserve punishment. Instead, God, your Maker, understands everything about you and loves you no matter what. He knows your weaknesses. When you pray to Him, you don't need to be afraid. You can tell Him about your struggles or your fears and what makes you happy or gives you joy. When you come before His throne, He will help you: He will supply your needs. When you are tempted to make a wrong choice, He will give you the strength to choose wisely.

Imagine that you are coming into the throne room of God. He is surrounded by angels who are calling out, "Holy, Holy, Holy is the Lord, God Almighty." He is aware that you have come, and He calls you by name. You approach and come forward. What will you say?

_____

_____

_____

What do you think God will say?

_____

_____

_____

What help do you need?

_____

_____

_____

Do you believe that God can help you?

_____

Use your answers to help you write today's prayer.

Today's prayer:

_____

_____

_____

_____

_____

_____

_____

THE REQUIREMENTS OF PRAYER OR THE BASICS OF PRAYER

Y ou can pray anytime and anywhere. You can pray about anything and everything. God will always hear you. He may answer your prayers by saying, "Yes," "Later," "No," "I will give you even more than what you have asked for," or "I have something else that is better."

When you pray, think about being in God's presence. If you were invited to see a great king, what would you do to get ready? There are things you can do to get ready to pray and things to do while you pray. These are called "requirements" or your part in prayer.

In Week Two, you will learn about five requirements of prayer.

1. A Clean Heart: Taking Care of Sin
2. Faith: Believing in God
3. Obedience: Doing God's Will
4. Praying in the Name of Jesus
5. Persistence: Not Giving Up

THE IMPORTANCE OF A CLEAN HEART

If I had enjoyed having sin in my heart, the Lord would not have listened. But God has listened. He has heard my prayer. —PSALM 66:18–19

What are you responsible for keeping clean?

_____

_____

_____

"I'll put my clothes away when it's time for Morgan to go home," Haley said to herself as she sprinted down the steps to greet her friend. This was not the first time that Haley had decided to put her things away later. Her bedroom was strewn about with shoes, socks, books, and other things. Her special drawing paper and pencils lay hidden beneath a pile of clothes on the floor.

"What do you want to do today?" Haley asked, as she motioned for her friend to come inside.

"Let's draw!" Morgan answered eagerly.

Bounding up the stairs by twos, Haley and Morgan raced into Haley's bedroom. Staring at the mess, Haley sighed. "Let me see now. Where are my special pencils and paper?" It took Haley a long time to find the paper and pencils.

A messy room is like having sin in our hearts and not taking care of it right away. Sin blocks our ears from hearing what God wants to say to us and sidetracks us from talking with God.

Ask God to show you the sins you need to clean out of your heart.

_____

_____

_____

As soon as you realize that you have sinned, get rid of the sin by telling God what you have done and ask Him to forgive you. This is called "confessing" your sins.

Below is a prayer to use as an example:

> Dear God,
> Yesterday, I was really angry with my little brother. He broke my favorite toy. I hit him and said some things that I should not have said. It was wrong. I ask for your forgiveness and for help to be able to love my brother even if he breaks my things. In Jesus' name, Amen.

After you pray, listen to see if there is anything that you should do. For example, if you told God that you had been fighting with your brother, He may tell you to tell your brother that you are sorry.

Using your answers, write your prayer on the next page.

Today's prayer:

_____

_____

_____

_____

_____

_____

_____

THE FAITH THAT RECEIVES

"Have faith in God," Jesus said. "So I tell you, when you pray for something, believe that you have already received it. Then it will be yours." —MARK 11:22, 24

Who do you have faith in?

_____

_____

_____

Antonio relished going to the park with his dad. The park had a jungle gym, slides, tunnels, and ropes to climb. It was Antonio's favorite place to be.

"Dad, will you take me to the park today?" he asked.

"I've got a few more things to do this morning, Antonio," his dad answered, looking up from his work. "But I'd love to go to the park with you this afternoon."

"Thanks Dad!" Antonio said, as he went to find his climbing shoes.

Antonio had faith in his dad. Antonio believed his dad would do as he said.

Jesus said, "Have faith in God." To have faith in God is to know God—to know what He wants for you. When you know what God wants for you, you can ask for it, believing that you have already received it.

For example, God wants you to grow in wisdom and knowledge and understanding. You can ask God for wisdom. Because you know He wants you to have wisdom, you can expect to receive it. You can ask God to give you courage to speak the truth, and expect to receive it because you know that God wants you to speak the truth at all times.

What do you have faith to ask God for?

_____

_____

_____

_____

Using your answers above, write your prayer below.

Today's prayer:

_____

_____

_____

_____

_____

_____

_____

OBEDIENCE: THE LIFE THAT CAN PRAY

Dear friends, if our hearts do not judge us, we can be bold with God. And he will give us anything we ask. That's because we obey his commands. We do what pleases him. . . . He has also commanded us to love one another. —1 JOHN 3:21–23

Did anyone ever say that you were bold? Take a few moments to remember what it felt like and write down what you did.

_____

_____

_____

_____

If not, would you like to be bold (without fear, having courage)?

_____

_____

_____

Kevin and Gabriel sat in the dugout waiting for their turn at bat.

Batter two, in the batter box," shouted Coach Steven. Kevin

timidly shuffled to the box. He had missed the last two practices. He nervously made circles in the dirt with his right foot as he waited for his turn.

"Batter up!" called the umpire.

With downcast eyes, Kevin stepped to the plate. As the balls sailed over home plate, the umpire shouted, "Strike one! Strike two! Strike three! You're out!"

Now it was Gabriel's turn. Gabriel swung his bat several times on the way to the batter's box. He had practiced a lot.

Once again the umpire called, "Batter up!"

Fixing his eyes on the pitcher, Gabriel took his position. As the ball sailed toward him, Gabriel stared at it and swung his bat hard. Crack! The bat hit the ball. Everyone watched the ball fly over the fence. Gabriel had hit a home run.

What do you think the difference was in the two batters?

_____

_____

_____

_____

You're right! One was bold and confident. The other lacked confidence. Confidence (boldness) is what you feel when you know you can do something; that is, you haven't told yourself you couldn't do it.

God wants us to come boldly to Him and ask for what we need. We can feel confident. Boldness and confidence come from knowing God, loving Him, knowing His love for us and desiring to do what pleases Him.

What do you want to boldly ask God for today?

_____

_____

_____

Today's prayer:

_____

_____

_____

_____

_____

_____

_____

PRAYING IN JESUS' NAME

> Until now you have not asked for anything in my name. Ask, and you will receive what you ask for. Then your joy will be complete. —JOHN 16:24

Who do you know that is important? What is his or her name?

_____

_____

_____

Perhaps you wrote the name of the president, your teacher, or parents, or someone else's name.

"Time to eat!" Connor called to Makayla and McKenzie, who were playing with their toys. Both girls looked at each other and kept right on playing. It was just their brother anyhow, and they didn't have to listen to *him*! A few moments later Connor called again, "Mom says it's time to eat!" Again Makayla and McKenzie looked at each other, but this time they put their dolls away and went in. The girls put their toys away because Connor spoke in his mother's name.

Similarly, Jesus gives you His name to use when you pray. Using

His name means that you are in agreement with what He wants. His name gives you authority before God to do and say what Jesus wants you to say.

The name of Jesus is the most powerful name that you can say. The Bible says that at the name of Jesus every knee will bow and every tongue will confess that He is Lord. There is great power in His name.

Using the name of Jesus means that you don't pray alone. Jesus prays with you. The Bible tells us that Jesus loves to pray with us.

What do you think Jesus would like you to ask the Father for in His name?

_____

_____

_____

_____

_____

Using your answers above, write your prayer below.

Today's prayer:

_____

_____

_____

_____

_____

_____

PRAYING WITH PERSISTENCE

Jesus told his disciples a story. He wanted to show them that they should always pray and not give up. —LUKE 18:1

Have you ever given up on doing something? _____

What was it?

_____

_____

_____

Last week, Sally thought the ground looked hard and dry. Now it was soft and fine. It was ready for planting. Sally dug a small hole. Then she got a seed out of her pocket. This particular seed was that of a pumpkin. Its flat oval shape and pale color did not look like it could turn into anything, but with confidence she placed the seed into the hole and covered it over with dirt. Every day she went out to see if there were any signs of growth. Although she could not see the seed, she did not stop taking care of it. She watered it and carefully pulled out weeds that tried to grow near where she had planted her seed. One morning, to her delight, she noticed a tiny plant begin to poke its way out of the ground. It was her pumpkin plant. As the days, weeks and months went by, Sally continued to water it and pull the weeds out from around her pumpkin plant. The plant got flowers, and then small pumpkins grew from their base. Sally knew that her plant would soon have large pumpkins on it.

Prayer is sometimes like a seed that you plant. Sometimes you can pray for a long time before you have the answer to your prayers and you may even feel like giving up. But don't. Jesus encouraged His disciples to keep on praying and not to give up.

There are many stories in the Bible about people who prayed for long periods of time without giving up. Once Daniel prayed for twenty-one days to understand something God was doing.*

Who or what have you prayed for a long time?

_____

_____

_____

An example of a prayer that you can pray and not give up on is that you might know God's love and be able to love everybody as He does. Or you could pray that you will never give up praying for those who do not know God.

Using your answers above, write your prayer below.

Today's prayer:

_____

_____

_____

_____

_____

_____

*See Daniel 10.

CLAIMING
GOD'S RICHES

The mail arrived early with a rainbow-colored envelope addressed to Monica. Glancing quickly toward the upper left-hand corner, Monica saw that it was from her favorite uncle. Excitedly she opened the envelope and read: "Dear Monica, Take this letter to REZ Toy Store and ask for the package with your name on it. Happy Birthday! Uncle Wally."

Monica could hardly wait to go. After checking with her mom, Monica raced off to REZ and asked for her package. Inside, she found something wonderful that she had been wanting for ages.

In Week Three you will learn that God has gifts waiting for you. All you need to do is ask for them and claim them. He doesn't think it's rude for you to ask. In fact, He delights in giving them to you.

ASKING FOR OURSELVES

So let us boldly approach the throne of grace. Then we will receive mercy. We will find grace to help us when we need it. —HEBREWS 4:16

Who helps you when you need help?

_____

What do they do?

_____

_____

_____

Feeling ashamed of his grade, Sammy crumpled his test paper and shoved it into the back of his desk. This was not the first time that he had failed a test since coming to his new school.

After school, he dug the paper out from the back corner of his desk and slowly moved his hands over it to smooth it out. As he walked toward his teacher's desk, he hoped that his teacher would understand. Sammy explained to his teacher that in his other school they had not covered these kinds of problems.

His teacher said, "Don't worry, Sammy. I understand how hard it can be in a new school. I remember what it was like to be a new student myself. If you come in before school next week, I will help you."

Feeling better, Sammy smiled as he walked back to his desk. He knew his teacher would help him.

So it is with God. He wants you to come to Him and share your needs. When you do, like Sammy, you will receive His help and kindness. (Hebrews 4:16 uses the words "grace" and "mercy" to describe God's help, acceptance, and kindness.)

When you are discouraged, impatient, feeling low, or have something heavy on your heart, take the time to tell God about it and listen to what He has to say.

Are there times when you need to know God's kindness and acceptance? When?

_____

_____

_____

Using your answer, write your prayer below.

Today's prayer:

_____

_____

_____

_____

_____

_____

_____

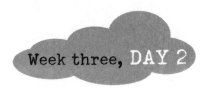

ASKING FOR GOOD THINGS

"Suppose your son asks for bread. Which of you will give him a stone? Or suppose he asks for a fish. Which of you will give him a snake? . . . How much more will your Father who is in heaven give good gifts to those who ask him!" —MATTHEW 7:9–12

What are some things you have asked others for, or things others have asked you for? How did you feel when you were able to give it to them, or when you received it?

_____

_____

_____

_____

The day was hot. The sun shone brightly, bouncing off of the pavement as Dylan, Michele, Courtney, Albert, and Russell raced their bicycles. Riding past Gabriel's house, they decided to stop and ask him for a cold glass of water. Do you think that Gabriel gave them stones instead? Or snakes? No, that would be silly for him to do. Gabriel was glad to give them each a tall cold glass of ice water.

Since God is so good, He is even more eager than our earthly friends to help you and to give you good things when you ask for them. He won't give you anything that could hurt you.

God has many good gifts to give you that you can ask Him for. Some of the gifts that He has for you are listed below. He delights in giving them to you.

Read each gift below and ask God to give it to you.

Wisdom: To be able to make the right choices. To tell the difference between right and wrong. "If any of you need wisdom, ask God for it. He will give it to you. God gives freely to everyone. He doesn't find fault" (James 1:5).

Peace: God's peace is a peace that can't be explained. "I leave my peace with you; I give my peace to you. I do not give it to you as the world does. Do not let your hearts be troubled and do not be afraid" (John 14:27).

Love: God's love that helps us to love even those who hurt us or others. "God has poured his love into our hearts. He did it through the Holy Spirit, whom he has given us" (Romans 5:5).

What gifts would you like God to give to you?

_____

_____

Using your answer, write your prayer below.

Today's prayer:

_____

Week three, DAY 3

GETTING WHAT WE ASK FOR

There is one thing we can be sure of when we come to God in prayer. If we ask anything in keeping with what he wants, he hears us. If we know that God hears what we ask for, we know that we have it. —1 JOHN 5:14–15

God promises that if we ask Him for anything that He wants for us, we will receive it. But how do we know what God wants us to have?

You can often know by reading the Bible. All of His promises to us can be found there.

You can also know what God wants for you by spending time with Him and asking Him to show you what you should do or what He wants for you.

The following story is about a young boy who did just that. Jeremiah didn't know what to do. It was his first day at his new church. The church was huge. It had 6,000 people in each service. There were so many people in the hallways after church that somehow he became separated from his mom and dad. He looked around to see if he could see them, but all he could see were feet. He wasn't tall enough to see above the people. At first he was afraid and began to panic, but then he stopped and prayed: "Dear God, What should I do? Where should I go?" He thought that God was telling him to go stand by the corner at the end of the hall. So he did. He got there just as his parents came around the corner and saw him.

Below are some of the things that we can have if we ask God for them:

- Courage to tell the truth and to do the right thing
- Help to control your temper when you are angry
- Forgiveness when you ask God to forgive you
- Wisdom (knowing what to do in every situation) when you ask God for it
- Love for those who make fun of you or tease you
- Peace instead of worry

Which of the above things do you want to ask God for today?

_____

_____

_____

Today's prayer:

_____

_____

_____

_____

_____

_____

_____

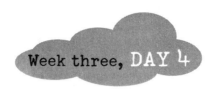

THE CURE FOR WORRY

Don't worry about anything. Instead, tell God about everything. Ask and pray. Give thanks to him. Then God's peace will watch over your hearts and minds because you belong to Christ Jesus. God's peace can never be completely understood. –PHILIPPIANS 4:6–7

What are some of the things that you have been told not to do?

Don't _____

Don't _____

Don't _____

God also tells us in the Bible not to do some things. Two of the things that He tells us not to do are lie and steal. There is one "don't," however, that He says more than any of the others and that is "Don't worry."

Leon rushed out the door worried that he might be late for his ball game. He slipped into the dugout just in time to hear his coach announce that he would need to cut someone from the team. Immediately, Leon began to worry about whether he would be the one. After practice, Leon remembered that he had not completed his science project. He worried that he might not have enough time to finish it. The more Leon worried, the more nervous he became.

Like Leon, do you worry? _____ What do you worry about?

_____

_____

_____

_____

Everybody worries. Instead of worrying, God tells us in Philippians to

- tell Him about everything,
- ask and pray about what makes us worry,
- give thanks.

Then God tells us, the opposite of worry—peace—will watch over our minds and hearts because we belong to Jesus.

Take a few moments to tell God about what makes you worry.

_____

_____

_____

_____

Today's prayer:

_____

_____

_____

_____

_____

_____

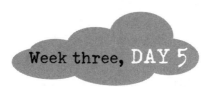

WHEN GOD SAYS "NO"

There is one thing we can be sure of when we come to God in prayer. If we ask anything in keeping with what he wants, he hears us. If we know that God hears what we ask for, we know that we have it. —1 JOHN 5:14–15

You also read today's verse on day three this week. If it is true that you can have whatever you ask God for as long as it is His will, it must also be true that if you ask God for what He doesn't want you to have, most likely you won't get it.

Have you ever been disappointed because you asked for something and did not get it? What was it?

_____

_____

Maria bounded into her house after a strenuous game of soccer. The aroma of freshly baked cookies filled the kitchen. She could almost taste the cookies with each breath.

"Mom, may I have a cookie?" she asked.

"No," her mother said. "The cookies are for after supper."

Maria couldn't believe it. She stomped off to take her shower. She was so hungry. Didn't her mother understand what it was like to come home from a game and want to eat?

Do you think that Maria's mother gave her the cookie after supper?

_____

Why do you think that Maria's mother did not want her to eat the cookie before supper?

_____

_____

Just as Maria's mother said "no" to Maria, God sometimes says "no" to what we ask for. Sometimes not getting what we ask for makes no sense to us. It may be years before we can look back and see that God knew best all along.

What have you prayed for and not gotten?

_____

_____

Today's prayer:
Dear God, help me to trust You when You say "no." Help me to see that You always want the best for me.

_____

_____

_____

_____

_____

_____

PRAYING FOR OTHERS

People who pray for others are called "intercessors." They see and hear about the needs of others, and turn those needs into prayers. They love others in the same way they love themselves.

Here are some characteristics of intercessors:

- They see what others need and then ask God for it.
- They don't stop praying until they see the answer.
- They pray for their friends, neighbors, school, city, state, country, and other countries.
- They know prayer makes a difference.
- They know when they ask God for something that God hears them.

In Week Four you will read about people who prayed for others.

PRAYING FOR OTHERS

Then Jesus said to them, "Suppose someone has a friend. He goes to him at midnight. He says, 'Friend, lend me three loaves of bread. A friend of mine on a journey has come to stay with me. I have nothing for him to eat.' Then the one inside answers, 'Don't bother me. The door is already locked. My children are with me in bed. I can't get up and give you anything.' I tell you, that person will not get up. And he won't give the man bread just because he is his friend. But because the man keeps on asking, he will get up. He will give him as much as he needs." —LUKE 11:5–8

Have you ever asked a friend for something? _____

What did you ask?

_____

_____

_____

Did your friend give it to you? _____

One day, I was making cookies with the neighbor children and discovered I did not have any flour. Kaitlin quickly said, "No problem! I'll go home and ask my mother for some." Although I didn't go with Kaitlin, I know that she pleaded with her mother to give her the flour.

"I can't give you flour now," her mother said. "I'm busy washing the floor."

But Kaitlin kept asking. Because she kept asking, her mother stopped and gave her the flour so she could give it to me. Kaitlin acted like the friend in today's Bible story. She didn't have the flour, but she knew her mother did. So, she pleaded with her for it. Jesus told His disciples the story in today's verses to teach them to pray for others and not to give up. Often my friends tell me about the things that are happening in their lives. They may tell me that one of their children is having a hard time in school. Although I can't help their child, I know who can, God. So, I begin to pray for him or her.

Praying for others is called "intercession." Jesus doesn't want us to give up praying for others.

Has anyone ever told you about their problems?

_____

What were they?

_____
_____
_____

Using your answer, ask God to help them.

Today's prayer:

_____

_____

_____

_____

_____

_____

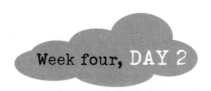

GOD SEEKS INTERCESSORS

> I looked for a man among them who would stand up for Jerusalem. I tried to find someone who would pray to me for the land. . . . But I could not find anyone who would pray for it. EZEKIEL 22:30

Did you ever ask someone to do something with you? _____

What was it?

_____

_____

_____

Maddie was thinking about all that had happened at school. She had overheard two girls talking about the new girl in school. "She can't even say a sentence without stuttering," they giggled.

Later in the day Maddie's friend said, "Please don't tell anybody, but my dad lost his job, and we may need to move."

During gym, Maddie saw Jimmy stick his leg out just as Sarah ran by. Sarah fell and scraped her knee. She glared at Jimmy. Jimmy snickered as he said to the teacher, "I didn't do anything."

Maddie knew that she could not change the things that had happened, but she could pray. God looks for those who will pray for people and for the land. Like Maddie, when you see things that are wrong, pray. The Bible tells us that Jesus loves to pray for us. When we pray we are joining Jesus.

Who did you see today that needed prayer?

_____

Is there anything happening in your neighborhood, school, city, state, country, or other countries that you could pray about?

_____

_____

_____

Use your answers above for the prayer below.

Today's prayer:

_____

_____

_____

_____

_____

_____

_____

Week four, DAY 3

THE LIMIT
OF INTERCESSION

First, I want all of you to pray for everyone. Ask God to bless them. Give thanks for them. Pray for kings. Pray for all who are in authority. —1 TIMOTHY 2:1-2A

Who are some of the people that you pray for?

_____

_____

_____

Olivia quietly sat by her desk while the Valentine cards were being passed out. Her teacher had placed a brightly decorated box covered with hearts of different sizes on her desk. She did not expect to receive any cards because this was her first day in the new school. As the children got up to pass out the cards, each one placed a card in her box. She couldn't believe it. Opening each one, she discovered that each of her classmates had written a note to welcome her to the class. Olivia's teacher had told the class that Olivia would be coming. The day before, the class had all made cards for Olivia.

Just as Olivia's teacher encouraged the children to give each one of their classmates a card, God tells us that we should pray for everyone. There is no one who is too good for prayer or too bad to pray for. Remember praying is also thanking God for the good things that you know are happening in someone's life.

Is there anyone that you don't feel like praying for? _____

Who?

_____

Ask God to bless them and give thanks for them.

God also wants you to pray for kings (those who are in charge, such as the president, mayor, governor, or teacher).

What is the president's name?

_____

Your mayor's name?

_____

Your teacher's name?

_____

Today's prayer:
Dear God, today I want to pray for President _____.
I ask that You give him wisdom. (Continue with your own prayer.)

_____

_____

_____

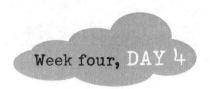

Week four, DAY 4

INTERCEDING FOR THOSE WHO CAN'T PRAY FOR THEMSELVES

My servant Job will pray for you. And I will accept his prayer. . . . —JOB 42:8

Have you ever not been able to do something for yourself?

_____

What was it?

_____

_____

Chloe arrived at school with a broken arm. Her three best friends gathered around asking, "What happened?" Chloe explained that she had fallen off her bike and had broken her arm in three places. She was worried about how to get her schoolwork done.

Lilly said, "Don't worry, Chloe. I'll carry your books for you between classes."

"I will get your lunch tray." Anna smiled.

"And I'll share my notes with you since you can't write with a

60

broken arm," said Sofia.

Chloe could not carry her books, her lunch tray, or write. She needed her friends' help. There are people you may know who need help but who do not believe in God. Although they need His help, they don't know they can pray and ask Him for it.

Do you know anyone who doesn't pray? _____

Who?

_____

Ask the Lord to show you what you can pray for them.

Today's prayer:

_____

_____

_____

_____

_____

_____

_____

PRAYING FOR THOSE WHO DO NOT KNOW GOD

With all my heart, I long for the people of Israel to be saved. —ROMANS 10:1

What have you ever wanted with all your heart?

_____

_____

_____

Caleb prayed as he knelt by his bed, "God, thank you for this day. Please bless my mommy and daddy and my sister, Abbie, and Grandma and Grandpa and Hoss, my dog. And, God, please take good care of Great-grandpa. I know he's loving being with You! Amen!" Caleb crawled under the covers and looked up at his mom. "Remember how we prayed and prayed for Great-grandpa to be saved?" he asked. "It seemed like he just never wanted to hear about Jesus. Sometimes it seemed like God was never going to answer. Sometimes I wanted to give up. It seemed like it was just no use to keep praying!"

Caleb's mom looked at him with love in her eyes and replied, "Yes, Caleb, I remember. God wants us to persist, to keep praying, especially when it's for something He wants too. We did. We kept praying for Great-grandpa, even when it didn't seem to be doing any good. I believe it was because of all those prayers that Great-grandpa accepted Jesus as his Savior a month before he died. Because we prayed and didn't give up, the way was made for Great-grandpa to go to be with Jesus when he died. Isn't that the most amazing and wonderful thing?"*

Like Caleb, Paul, the writer of today's verse, longed for the people of Israel to be saved. Paul wanted them to know God for themselves, and not just know things about Him.

Who do you know that does not yet know God?

_____

Commit to pray for them and be ready when they say, "Yes, I want to be a Christian."

If you have not yet become a Christian, find someone to talk to and then pray the prayer found in the back of this book. Ask God to put in you a desire to know Him and to love Him.

Today's prayer:

_____

_____

_____

_____

_____

_____

*Story from Dawn Morley, Pebbles and Stones leader.

PRAYER AS A WAY OF LIFE

Micah watched the river flowing peacefully past her family's cabin in the woods. It sparkled as it rippled on its way to the great lake. When it was swollen from heavy rain, it rushed by, sounding like thunder. Most evenings, after the sun had set and the sky grew dark, the banks of the river were outlined by moonlight and stars. Micah could still see the river was there. On nights when the clouds covered the stars, Micah could hear the river flowing even though she couldn't see it. No matter what time of day it was, Micah knew the river was there.

Just as Micah knew the river was always there even when she could not see it, God wants you to know that He is always with you. In Week Five, you will learn that prayer is more than something you do; it is being with God.

PRAYER AS A CONVERSATION WITH GOD

> Then the man and his wife heard the Lord God walking in the garden. It was the coolest time of the day. They hid from the Lord God among the trees of the garden.
> —GENESIS 3:8

Who do you like to talk with the most?

_____

What do you like to talk about?

_____

_____

The first two people God created were named Adam and Eve. It is clear from the Bible that God talked and walked with them. What do you think they talked about?

_____

_____

_____

What would you have talked to God about? What questions would you have asked Him?

_____

_____

_____

_____

One day Brittany's mom asked her to read to her sister. She did for a while and then became bored. She wished she was playing soccer. Shoving the book into her sister's hands, Brittany picked up her soccer ball. She began tossing it from one hand to the other, throwing it harder and higher each time. Then the ball flew so high it bounced off the ceiling, hit the wall, and knocked her mother's favorite vase to the floor with a loud crash.

"What's going on in there?" her mother called.

Brittany found a place to hide by saying, "Erin knocked your vase off the table." As soon as she said that, Brittany began to feel different on the inside.*

When Adam and Eve disobeyed God, like Brittany, they too became afraid and hid in a lie. God called them to come out of their hiding place and asked, "Where are you?" Just as God called out to Adam and Eve, He continues to call out to all of us. "Come and talk to me," He calls. He likes to hear our voices and loves to have us talk to Him.

Are you sometimes too busy to talk to God or just simply don't want to? _____

Talk to God right now about it. Ask Him to help you learn how to hear His voice.

Today's prayer:

_____

_____

_____

_____

_____

_____

_____

*Story taken from *Hiding Places* by Kathleen Trock, copyright 2009.

LIVING PRAYERFULLY

Never stop praying. —1 THESSALONIANS 5:17

A friend of mine ties a string around her finger to remind herself of what she needs to do. Do you do something to help yourself remember? _____

What?

_____

"Spread your feet, bend your knees, stay low to the ground, keep your glove down, and always watch the ball go into your glove," instructed Alex's coach. "When I look at you on the field, I want to see the button of your hat, not your face." Over and over, Coach gave the same directions for fielding the ball, and Alex caught, and missed, hundreds of balls during his practices. By the time of the first game, Alex didn't need to think about how to field the ball. Catching it had become a part of him.

God wants prayer to be a part of us, something that we don't have to think about doing. God whispers to us, "Pray, pray, pray." Throughout the day and even in our dreams, He whispers. He wants us to pray. He opens our spiritual eyes to see what we should pray for; He opens our ears to hear what we should pray. Prayer is God's idea.

Remember, prayer is talking with God.

Today's verse encourages you never to stop praying. Let prayer become a natural thing you do. Below are a few suggestions to help you become an always "pray-er."

- Choose a prayer place. It may be a chair, in a corner, or in a tree.
- Pray before you get out of bed in the morning.
- Pray before you go to bed at night.
- Pray when you hear good news.
- Pray when you hear bad news.
- Pray whenever you see someone having a hard time.
- Pray when you hear a police siren or an ambulance.
- Pray when you hear someone is sick.
- Pray when you are getting dressed.
- (Fill in your own ideas here.)

_____

_____

_____

Today's prayer:

_____

_____

_____

_____

_____

_____

_____

HEARING FROM HEAVEN

My sheep listen to my voice. I know them, and they fol-
low me. —JOHN 10:27

Whose voices can you recognize without seeing their faces?

_____

_____

The phone rang as Erica came into the house. Her mother answered it and laughed with joy. Handing the phone to Erica, her mother said, "Somebody wants to talk with you."

"Hello?" Erica said. Breaking into a big smile, Erica recognized the voice of her favorite aunt.

Just as Erica was able to recognize her aunt's voice, so God wants us to recognize His voice. The following Bible story is from 1 Samuel 3:1–10. It's about Samuel, a young boy, and a priest named Eli, who both served the Lord in the temple. Samuel learned to hear and recognize God's voice.

In those days the Lord didn't give many messages or visions to His people. One night Eli was lying down in his usual place. His eyes were becoming so weak he couldn't see very well. Samuel was lying down in the Lord's house. That's where the ark of God was kept. The lamp of God was still burning. The Lord called out to Samuel. Samuel ran over to Eli and said, "Here I am. You called out to me."

But Eli said, "I didn't call you. Go back and lie down."

So he went and lay down. Again the Lord called out, "Samuel!"

Samuel got up and went to Eli. He said, "Here I am. You called me."

"My son," Eli said, "I didn't call you. Go back and lie down."

The Lord called to Samuel for the third time. Samuel got up and went to Eli. He said, "Here I am. You called me."

Then Eli realized that the Lord was calling the boy. So Eli told Samuel, "Go and lie down. If someone calls you again, say, 'Speak, Lord, I'm listening.'"

So Samuel went and lay down in his place. The Lord came and stood there. He called out just as He had done the other times. He said, "Samuel! Samuel!"

Then Samuel replied, "Speak, I am listening."

God is always speaking to us, but sometimes like Samuel, we may not realize that it is Him. Remember:
- God's voice will always be truthful.
- God's voice will always be loving.
- God's voice will always agree with the Bible.

Have you ever heard God speak? _____

What did He He say?

_____

What would you like to talk to God about?

_____

_____

Today's prayer:

Dear God, I want to hear Your voice and recognize it as the voice of my best friend. Teach me to hear Your voice.

_____

_____

_____

_____

_____

_____

_____

PRAY THE ORDINARY

At all times, pray by the power of the Spirit. Pray all kinds of prayers. Be watchful, so that you can pray. Always keep on praying for all of God's people.
—EPHESIANS 6:18

Underline every word "all" and "always" in the above verse. There are four: all the time, all kinds of prayer, always keep on praying, and pray for all of God's people.

Ryan honked the van horn one more time, hoping his mom would get the message. He, his brother, and his sister were anxious to get going. Finally, Mom got in the driver's seat and put the key into the ignition.

"What took you so long?" asked Ryan.

His mom looked at him and replied, "I'm sorry, Ryan, I didn't mean to keep you all waiting, but Christa had a problem. She asked if I would pray for her. I didn't want to forget, so I prayed with her right there over the phone."

Ryan responded, "You're always praying about everything! Someone is sick, you pray. There's a flood in Africa, you pray. Your friend is sad, you pray. You get good news, you pray. You lose your keys, you pray. Is there anything you won't pray about?"

"God wants us to pray about everything!" Ryan's mom said. "Nothing is too big or too small for Him. If it's important to us or to someone else—it's important to Him! We can always go to Him; it shows that we trust Him and that we know He is the one who is in control."*

In 1 Thessalonians 5:17, God tells us to pray at all times. In today's verse He adds, pray at all times, by the power of the Spirit. When we pray, it's important to remember that it's not our power that brings the answers; the answers will always come through God's Spirit.

How are you doing at remembering to pray all the time?

_____

_____

Who are you praying for?

_____

_____

_____

Today's prayer:

_____

_____

_____

_____

_____

_____

*Story from Dawn Morley, Pebbles and Stones leader.

A PRIVATE MEETING WITH THE FATHER

When you pray, go into your room. Close the door and pray to your Father, who can't be seen. He will reward you. Your Father sees what is done secretly. —MATTHEW 6:6

Aaron was looking forward to going fishing with his dad, just the two of them. They had planned the trip months ago. Now, it had to be postponed. Sadness covered Aaron like a blanket. Aaron and his dad loved being together. Sometimes they would laugh at the silliest things until their stomachs ached. There were other times when they talked about serious things.

Who do you like to spend time alone with?

_____

Where do you go?

_____

Just as Aaron liked going off alone with his dad, God encourages us to spend time alone with Him. When He tells us to shut the door, He is asking us to shut out all of the distractions that take us away from being with Him. As we make being alone with God number 1, we will discover more and more about God, ourselves, and others. We will learn how we should live. We will also discover how much God delights in us.

Jesus often went off by Himself to be alone with God. When His disciples went looking for Him, they often found Him praying.

When you want to be alone with God, where do you go?

_____

I have a special chair in my house that I like to sit in when I want to be alone with God. As I sit there, I often read the Bible and listen to what God wants to say to me as I read.

Today's prayer:

_____

_____

_____

_____

_____

_____

_____

Week Six

MODEL PRAYERS OF THE BIBLE

The Bible is overflowing with prayers. One such conversation with God is the prayer of King Solomon. He became the wisest king who ever lived because he asked God for wisdom. Another prayer is the prayer of Elijah who prayed that it would not rain for three years, and it didn't. King David asked God to search him to see if there was any sin in him. Their prayers show us that Solomon, Elijah, and David knew God. They knew that God was with them and would help them. Their prayers are models for us to use when we pray.

In Week Six you will read some of their prayers and discover the importance of prayer in their lives and in their friendship with God.

OUR LORD'S MODEL PRAYER

"Our Father in heaven, hallowed (kept holy) be your name, your kingdom come, your will be done on earth as it is in heaven. Give us today our daily bread. Forgive us our debts, as we also have forgiven our debtors. And lead (bring) us not into temptation, but deliver us from the evil one." For yours is the kingdom and the power and the glory forever. Amen. —MATTHEW 6:9-13, NIV

There are a lot of things that we need to learn to do. What have you asked someone to teach you?

_____

Melanie watched her older brother blow bubbles, huge bubbles. His bubbles were so large that they covered his face when they burst. He was the best bubble blower in the whole neighborhood. On lazy summer afternoons, he would sit with his friends under the maple tree and have a bubble-blowing contest. Melanie would blow the whistle to start the contest. First, they would chew, chew, chew, and then, when the gum was soft enough, they would get their mouth in the right position and begin to blow. Her brother always won.

Although Melanie was four years younger than her brother, she wanted to blow bubbles like his. She asked him to teach her, and she watched him and practiced doing what he did. That's how Melanie learned to blow bubbles that covered her face.

When Jesus' disciples wanted to learn how to do something Jesus did, they watched Him. He did many miracles. They saw Him multiply food, heal the sick, raise the dead, and give sight to the blind and hearing to the deaf. They also watched and heard Him pray. Of all the things that they saw Jesus do, the only thing that they asked Him to teach them was how to pray. The prayer that Jesus taught them is called the "Lord's Prayer."

The Lord's Prayer teaches these things:
- That God is your Father
- That you are His child
- That you need to worship and honor Him
- To pray for God's will to be done on earth just as it is being done in heaven
- To ask God to give you and others what they need
- To ask God to forgive your sins and to lead you away from being tempted to sin
- To ask God to help you forgive others

Before you pray the Lord's Prayer, take time to write the answers to the following questions:

Who is God?

_____

What is special about His name?

_____

How are things in heaven?

_____

Are there sick people there?

_____

Do people hurt other people in heaven?

_____

Is there teasing in heaven?

_____

What would it be like if God's will was always done all the time on earth as it is in heaven?

_____

_____

_____

What needs do you have today?

_____

Do you need to ask God to forgive you of anything? _____ If your answer is yes, why not stop right now and ask for God's forgiveness.

Do you need to forgive anyone? _____

Today's prayer: (You may put someone's name in the blank spaces.)

Our Father in heaven, hallowed [kept holy] be Your name, Your kingdom come, Your will be done on earth as it is in heaven. Give _____ this day his/her daily bread. And forgive me or him/her for _____ debts, as we also have forgiven _____ debtors. And lead [bring] _____ not into temptation, but deliver _____ from the evil one. For Yours is the kingdom and the power and the glory forever. Amen.

*Concept from Pebble and Stones training on prayer.

Week six, DAY 2

A PRAYER TO KNOW GOD'S LOVE

I bow in prayer to the Father because of my work among you. From the Father his whole family in heaven and on earth gets its name. I pray that he will use his glorious riches to make you strong. May his Holy Spirit give you his power deep down inside you. Then Christ will live in your hearts because you believe in him. And I pray that your love will have deep roots. I pray that it will have a strong foundation. May you have power with all God's people to understand Christ's love. May you know how wide and long and high and deep it is. And may you know his love, even though it can't be known completely. Then you will be filled with everything God has for you. —EPHESIANS 3:14–19

Who loves you the most?

_____

How do you know?

_____

Isabella sat with her hands crisscrossed to cover the stains on the front of her freshly washed T-shirt. She placed one shoe on top of the toe of the other one, hoping to conceal a gaping hole in it. Her socks sagged around her ankles. This morning she could not find any rubber bands to hold them up. She wished she had socks and hair bows to match her dresses, like the other girls had.

Isabella felt uncomfortable sitting next to the neatly dressed children, but she loved hearing her Sunday school teacher talk. Just then Isabella heard her teacher say, "God loves *you*!" Her teacher started each class with these words. Isabella didn't really believe that God loved her; after all she was so poor that sometimes her family did not have enough food to eat, and her father had not been able to find a job for months.

During journaling time, one of her classmates said that God had been talking to her about the poor and telling her how much He loved them. Her classmate had tears in her eyes as she said over again, "God really loves the poor and wants us to help them. He wants me to bring some food to our church pantry. I am going to use my allowance money this week to buy some canned goods."

Isabella couldn't believe what she was hearing: "God loves the poor." And she was poor. "God, do you really love me?" she wondered.

From inside, Isabella heard God say over and over again, "I love you, Isabella."

Like Isabella, you may have heard the words "God loves you" many times, but you may have thought that it wasn't true for you.

Before you begin to pray for others today, ask God to help *you* know His love. Ask God to show you others who need to know that God loves them, and then pray this prayer or your own prayer for them.

Today's prayer:
Dear God, I bow in prayer to you. I pray that _____ will know how much You love them. Help them to know there is no end to Your love. May they be filled with Your nature so that they will always make right choices. May You fill them with everything that You have for them.

_____

_____

_____

_____

_____

_____

_____

Week six, DAY 3

A PRAYER FOR SPIRITUAL RICHES

That's why we have not stopped praying for you. We have been praying for you since the day we heard about you. We have been asking God to fill you with the knowledge of what he wants. We pray that he will give you spiritual wisdom and understanding. We pray that you will lead a life that is worthy of the Lord. We pray that you will please him in every way. So we want you to bear fruit in every good thing you do. We want you to grow to know God better. We want you to be very strong, in keeping with his glorious power. We want you to be patient. Never give up. Be joyful as you give thanks to the Father. —COLOSSIANS 1:9–12A

Did you ever start to do something that you knew God didn't want you to do, and then stopped before you did it? Why did you stop?

_____

_____

_____

"Remember to pray!" Samantha's teacher's words drifted from Samantha's thoughts as unnoticed as a leaf falling from a tree. Praying had never been easy for Samantha. She often didn't know what to pray, so it was hard for her to remember to pray. Today she walked over to her friend's house. She saw her friend Mandy waiting as she skipped up the driveway.

"What took you so long?" Mandy asked. "Don't you remember what we've planned for today?"

Samantha remembered and her stomach felt tight. They were going to the store to steal a bag of candy. It was all planned out. Mandy would distract the clerk while Samantha slipped the candy into her oversized pockets. As Mandy went over the plan again, Samantha's teacher's words poked into her thoughts: "Remember to pray."

"What should I do, God? What should I say to Mandy?" Samantha prayed. Turning to Mandy she said, "I think this is a bad idea. Let's ride our bikes instead."

Do you think that Mandy rode bikes with Samantha? _____

If Mandy continued to press Samantha to go to the store, do you think Samantha would have gone? _____

Why?

_____

The following week, Samantha's teacher told her that she had been praying for her to know God's will. Samantha smiled as she shared what had happened.

The apostle Paul wrote a letter to the Christians living in Colossae, reminding them to remember to pray for each other. He asked them to pray for these spiritual riches for each other:

- To know God's will
- To live to please God
- To be patient and full of joy in hard times
- To give thanks to God

Today's prayer:
Ask God to show you one person to pray for today. Pray this prayer from Colossians for them.

Dear God, I ask You to fill _____ with the knowledge of what You want. I ask that You give _____ spiritual wisdom and understanding. I pray that _____ will lead a life that is worthy of You. I pray that _____ will please You in every way. So _____ will bear fruit in every good thing he/she does. I want _____ to grow to know You better. I want _____ to be very strong, in keeping with Your glorious power. I want _____ to be patient. Never give up. Be joyful as he/she gives thanks to You, Father God.

A PRAYER TO KNOW GOD BETTER

I pray to the God of our Lord Jesus Christ. God is the glorious Father. I keep asking him to give you the wisdom and understanding that come from the Holy Spirit. I want you to know God better. I also pray that your mind might see more clearly. Then you will know the hope God has chosen you to receive. You will know that the things God's people will receive are rich and glorious. And you will know his great power. It can't be compared with anything else. It is at work for us who believe. It is like the mighty strength God showed when he raised Christ from the dead. —EPHESIANS 1:17–20A

As his family drove into the new neighborhood where they were moving, Aaron noticed many children playing outside. Some were riding their bicycles while others gathered in a front yard to play soccer. Aaron had heard that this was a neighborhood full of children. His cousins, who lived there, had even told him some of the children's names. He'd heard that Samuel was the best soccer player, not only in the neighborhood but also in the school. He also knew that Sharon liked to draw and her driveway was always covered with chalk drawings. Although Aaron knew about these children, He did not know them. Over the next several months, Aaron got to know the kids; he played soccer with Samuel and learned for himself that Samuel was the best soccer player in the neighborhood. He also learned more about Sharon as they drew chalk pictures together. Aaron discovered she wasn't afraid to hold insects. She even kept a pet grasshopper in a jar under her bed.

You may have heard Bible stories about God, but you may not know Him for yourself. That's just how it was for Aaron, hearing stories about children in his new neighborhood before he got to know them for himself. Hearing stories about God from the Bible is not enough. The writer of the Bible verse today prays that we might know God Himself, not just know *about* Him. (If you need help to do this, turn to the ABCs of Salvation in the back of this book.)

Just as Aaron got to know the children on his street by being with them, you get to know God by praying (talking to Him about your thoughts and feelings and the needs of others) and listening on the inside to hear what He is saying to you.

Who do you think needs to know God? _____

Pray this prayer for them:

Today's prayer:
I pray that _____ and _____ will know You more. I also pray that their hearts (the place of our emotions) would be full of Your hope. Let them know what You want them to do.

May they always think about the good things that You have for them and experience the great power that You have given Your people, the power of Your love.

A PRAYER FOR BLESSING

Jabez cried out to the God of Israel. He said, "I wish you would bless me. I wish you would give me more territory. Let your powerful hand be with me. Keep me from harm. Then I won't have any pain." God gave him what he asked for. —1 CHRONICLES 4:10

Have you ever been kept from harm? _____ If you were, that is called being blessed. What happened?

_____

_____

_____

_____

In Africa, a group of children were traveling in a van to a small village. They wanted to tell those who lived there how much God loved them. The driver of the van took a wrong turn and drove into a dangerous area. The driver tried to find his way to safety, but with each turn he became more lost. Finally, the van ran out of gas. The children prayed and asked God what they should do. They sensed that God wanted them to get out of the van and to run in a certain direction. So they did. They came upon a road just as a United Nations convoy came by. The convoy stopped and carried them to safety. God kept them from harm.

Jabez lived during Old Testament times, more than 2,000 years ago. Jabez asked God to bless him; that is, to cause him to have favor with God and others. Jabez also asked God to enlarge his territory, both his land and his area of influence. Some of the most influential people are leaders in government like the president and governor. There are leaders in all areas, in sports, music, art, or in schools. These are all exceptional places of influence, but the greatest place of influence on earth is to tell others about God's plan to save them. Ask God to help you share His story with others. You can also ask God to set you free from thoughts that hold you back from being who God created you to be, a child of excellence. Next, Jabez asked that God's hand would be with him. His prayer, "Let your powerful hand be with me," creates a picture of a hand that is ready and willing to help us, strengthen us, and direct us. Finally, Jabez prayed that he would be kept from harm.

What are you afraid of that may harm you?

_____

_____

_____

Jabez prayed and God answered him. May his prayer for blessing become your prayer for the rest of your life and may you experience God's answers to it daily.

Today's prayer:

Dear God, I ask You to bless me. I ask You to give me more territory. Let Your powerful hand be with me. Keep me from harm. Then I won't have any pain.

_____

_____

_____

_____

_____

_____

_____

HEROES OF PRAYER

When I was growing up, I had several heroes and heroines. A hero or heroine is someone we admire because of his or her bravery or great feats and deeds. It is someone we want to be like. One of my prayer heroines is Gladys Aylward, a missionary to China, who led hundreds of children out of danger and into safety.

Looking through the Bible, there are several people who I consider to be prayer heroes. They knew and loved God and prayed for His will to be done. In Week Seven, you will read about their lives and the prayers they prayed.

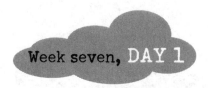
JESUS, THE MAN WHO PRAYED THE BEST

It was very early in the morning and still dark. Jesus got up and left the house. He went to a place where he could be alone. There he prayed. —MARK 1:35

But Jesus often went away to be by himself and pray. —LUKE 5:16

On one of those days, Jesus went out to a mountainside to pray He spent the night praying to God. —LUKE 6:12

Do you like to be alone? _____ Why do you think Jesus often went off by Himself to pray?

_____

The disciples of Jesus (those who watched Him, followed Him, and wanted to be like Him) noticed that Jesus often went off alone to pray. He prayed in the morning and in the evening. He prayed on mountaintops, in gardens, and indoors. Jesus prayed before He chose His twelve disciples. He prayed when He was led into the wilderness and while He was there. He prayed on the cross, and

He prayed as He went up into heaven. Why did He pray so much? Jesus told us that He never did anything unless He saw His Father doing it first, and He never said anything unless He first heard His Father saying it. Jesus prayed to find out what God wanted Him to do. Jesus knew what to say and do because He spent time praying and talking with God.

In the Lord's Prayer, Jesus tells us to pray for God's will to be done. Jesus knew God's will because He spent time in prayer. God wants to show you His will too. As you spend time in prayer, He will show you.

Where will you go to be alone with God?

_____

I suggest that you get a journal, a notebook, to write about the times you spend with God.

Today's prayer:

_____

_____

_____

_____

_____

_____

_____

Week seven, DAY 2

PAUL, THE MAN WHO PRAYED CONSTANTLY

God knows that I always remember you in my prayers.
—ROMANS 1:9B–10A

We always thank God, the Father of our Lord Jesus Christ,
when we pray for you. . . . That's why we have not stopped
praying for you. —COLOSSIANS 1:3, 9A

Night and day I always remember you in my prayers.
—2 TIMOTHY 1:3B

What have you prayed for the longest?

_____

How long did you pray?

_____

In Namibia, a group of children live in a humble orphanage. There is
no electricity and no television. They often eat only one meal a day.
Before living in the orphanage, these children lived in the dumps

outside their village. There they fought off animals for the scraps of food they found among the trash, and they slept wherever they could find shelter in the shadows of the trees. A few years ago, I was invited to visit them. I asked their guardian, "Do the children like to pray?"

With a smile that quickly spread across her face she answered, "Yes, the children love to pray. They seem to pray all the time. They pray without me reminding them to pray."

"Could we pray together?" I asked.

"Yes, of course!" she said, as she called the children. There were ninety-nine children in the orphanage. As they began to pray, many of the children lay on the dirt floor. While they prayed, small mud puddles of tears began to form on the floor as they prayed.

"What are they praying for?" I asked.

"They are praying for the other children, those who still live in the dumps who have no one to care for them. They pray that they will find food for today. They pray that the orphanage will find room for their friends."

These children prayed like Paul. They prayed for the other children because they loved them. They wanted the other children to live and to know God's love.

Read the following Scriptures again:
- "God knows that I always remember you in my prayers" (Romans 1:9b–10a).
- "We always thank God, the Father of our Lord Jesus Christ when we pray for you. . . .That's why we have not stopped praying for you" (Colossians 1:3, 9b).
- "Night and day I always remember you in my prayers" (2 Timothy 1:3b).

Ask God to give you a love for others, so that you might pray as Paul and these children did—full of His love.

Today's prayer:

_____

_____

_____

_____

_____

_____

_____

ELIJAH, AN ORDINARY MAN WHO PRAYED POWERFULLY

The prayer of a godly person is powerful. It makes things happen. Elijah was just like us. He prayed hard that it wouldn't rain. And it didn't rain on the land for three and a half years. Then he prayed again. That time it rained. And the earth produced its crops.

—JAMES 5:16B–18

You can read the full story of Elijah's prayer in 1 Kings 17:1–7 and 18:1–46.

What prayers has God answered for you?

_____

_____

_____

_____

The Bible is filled with stories about ordinary people doing great things. The Bible promises that those who know God will do great things in His name. Elijah was such a man. He prayed that it would not rain for three and a half years and it didn't. Then he prayed again, this time asking for rain and it started to rain. It wasn't that Elijah had the power to make it rain or stop it from raining. It was because he earnestly prayed according to God's will.

Samone and Mary looked at each other as they heard the siren blowing. It had been windy all morning, and the wind was getting gustier. Both Samone and Mary knew that this time the school's siren was not another practice drill. It was for real.

"Quickly, class," Mrs. Bee said, "get into line! We're going to the shelter."

As they hurried toward the shelter, Mary heard her friend Samone praying, "Dear God, keep us safe and help us not to be afraid." Sitting on mats, Mary huddled closer to her friend. She felt safer there as Samone kept on praying.

Mary and Samone liked doing a lot of things together. They giggled at cartoons, made up songs, and rode their bicycles. They both liked the color purple and orange soda pop. They even had identical brown, curly haircuts. Their other friends often told them they looked like twins. There was one difference, however. Samone knew and loved God. She prayed, and God heard her. Mary did not think that God would hear her prayers.

Like Mary, have you ever thought you couldn't pray because you weren't special enough? _____ Prayer is not about being special; prayer is about believing God and choosing His ways. Ask God to help you learn to pray powerfully like Elijah.

Today's prayer:

_____

_____

_____

_____

_____

_____

_____

JEHOSHAPHAT, THE MAN WHO PRAYED FOR VICTORY

(Jehoshaphat) said: "O Lord, God of our fathers, are you not the God who is in heaven? You rule over all the kingdoms of the nations. Power and might are in your hand, and no one can withstand you. O our God, will you not judge them? For we have no power to face this huge army that is attacking us. We do not know what to do, but our eyes are upon you." —2 CHRONICLES 20:6, 12 NIV

Who is the most powerful person that you know?

_____

What can that person do?

_____

What are some things he or she can't do?

_____

_____

Jehoshaphat was a very powerful king. One day King Jehoshaphat learned that a large army was planning an attack against his kingdom. Even though he was king, Jehoshaphat knew that he could not defeat this great army. So he called all the people together, the young and the old, to fast and pray. As they fasted and prayed, God spoke and told them that He would fight for them.

There are several things that we can learn about prayer from Jehoshaphat:

- King Jehoshaphat had a problem that was too big for him, and he was afraid.
- He gathered everyone together, the fathers and mothers, grandparents and children, even babies, to ask God for help. Prayer is for everyone.
- He talked to God while everyone stood before God together.
- He praised God and said how strong God was.
- He told God that he did not know what to do.
- He asked God to help.
- He waited for God to answer.

You can do what Jehoshaphat did when you have a problem that's too big for you:

- Admit that the problem is too big for you.
- Ask others to pray with you.
- Wait for God's answer.
- Thank Him for the answer.*

Can you think of a problem that's too big for you?

_____

_____

If so, who could you ask to pray with you?

_____

Tell them what the problem is, and then ask them to pray with you.

Today's prayer:

_____

_____

_____

_____

_____

_____

_____

*Concept from _Guide to Happiness_, a Pebbles and Stones curriculum, copyright 2007.

DAVID, THE MAN WHO PRAYED AND CONFESSED SIN

Wash me. Then I will be whiter than snow. Let me hear you say, "Your sins are forgiven." That will bring me joy and gladness. —PSALM 51:7B, 8A

Read 2 Samuel 11:1–12:23.

Have you ever done something and felt bad about it later? _____

What was it?

_____

_____

"Don't forget! Come home right away!" Jacob's mother called after him as he ran out the door for school.

Jacob sighed. His sister's concert was after school. He didn't want to hear her piano solo. He'd already heard her practice a thousand times. Besides he wanted to go to Bobby's house after school to practice for their soccer game. What could he do?

On their way to school, Jacob and Bobby came up with a great plan. They would go to Bobby's house after school. Jacob would call his mother from Bobby's house and tell her that he'd forgotten that he had to stay after school to practice for the school play. Of course, she would understand. The plan was a success.

But as soon as Jacob got home later that evening, he got a gnawing feeling inside. He wondered if his mother could tell that he had lied. During dinner, Jacob's mother asked him how play practice went. Jacob looked down at his lap as he said, "It was great. I even remembered all my lines." As soon as the words came out of his mouth, that same gnawing feeling began again. Jacob tossed and turned as he tried to fall asleep, but the gnawing feeling kept him awake. Jacob began to pray, "Dear God, I lied to my mother today, and I am feeling bad." As Jacob continued to talk to God about his lie, he began to feel better. He got out of bed and told his mother what he had done.

Telling God about our sins is called "confession." When we confess our sins, we tell God about the wrong we have done and ask Him to forgive us. He promises that He always forgives. As David said, confessing will bring us gladness and joy again.

Spend some time today asking God to cleanse you, to make you free from sin, and give you the desire to obey Him.

Today's prayer:
Dear God, You know all about me. You know how hard it is for me to _____. I am sorry for _____. Help me not to _____ anymore. I want to have a pure heart that always chooses to do what is right in Your sight.

_____

_____

Week Eight

THE DIFFERENCE PRAYER MAKES

During Week Eight, you will read about the difference prayer makes in the lives of those who prayed and the people they prayed for.

Seven weeks ago, Tommy asked the question, "What's the good of prayer anyhow?" Have you discovered the answer during the past weeks?

In Week Eight you will have the opportunity to reflect on how you have become a part of God's story through your prayers.

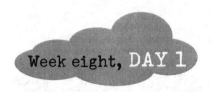

PRAYER RELEASES GOD'S POWER

The prayer of a godly person is powerful. It makes things happen. —JAMES 5:16B

Who do you know who gets things done?

_____

What have they done?

_____

Rebecca watched the grass in her neighborhood turn more brown every week. She heard on the news that no one was allowed to water their yards because it had not rained for months and the city's water supply was nearly gone. While Rebecca was thinking about how brown the grass was, she remembered this Bible verse, "The prayer of a godly person is powerful. It makes things happen."

Rebecca asked her friends to pray with her for rain. They promised each other that they would pray every day for rain until it rained. Within a week, it rained. Rebecca and her friends praised and thanked God.

God tells us in the Bible that the prayer of a godly person (one who knows God) is powerful. His or her prayers help make things happen. Because God is powerful, prayers are powerful.

Like Rebecca, what things have you noticed that you could pray about in your home?

_____

In your school?

_____

In your neighborhood?

_____

Your city?

_____

Your country?

_____

Today's prayer:

_____

_____

_____

_____

_____

_____

_____

THE KEY TO GREAT WORKS

What I'm about to tell you is true. Anyone who has faith in me will do what I have been doing. In fact, he will do even greater things. That is because I am going to the Father. And I will do anything you ask in my name. Then the Son will bring glory to the Father. –JOHN 14:12–13

Did anyone ever tell you that you could do what they were doing?

_____

What was it?

_____

_____

_____

Orlo quietly watched his uncle select a small block of wood. Holding the wood in one hand and a knife in the other, his uncle began to cut into the wood. As he made gouges of different sizes and shapes, the wood began to look like a dog. Looking at Orlo's smiling face, his uncle said, "Orlo, you will be able to make even better carvings than I do, because you will begin to learn earlier than I did, and I will teach you everything I can."

Like Orlo, the disciples (the followers of Jesus) watched Jesus do many things. They saw Him multiply food so there was enough for everyone to eat. They saw Him heal the sick, make blind people see, and make deaf people hear. They even saw Him stop a thunderstorm. Before Jesus returned to heaven, He promised His disciples that if they believed in Him, they would do even greater things than He had done.

God wants to work through you when you pray. Ask God what He would like to do through your prayers?

_____

_____

_____

Today's prayer:
Dear God, thank You for showing me to pray

_____

_____

_____

I ask

_____

_____

_____

In Jesus' name, Amen.

THE STRENGTH TO STAND

Finally, let the Lord make you strong. Depend on his mighty power. —EPHESIANS 6:10

Take a minute now to read Ephesians 6:10–20.
Have you ever done anything to make yourself stronger?

_____

Maybe you started exercising or eating healthier foods. What did you do?

_____

_____

Sepia's class had just finished reading biographies of several authors. Their new assignment was to write their own biography and read it in front of the class. Sepia was nervous. She hated to get up in front of everyone and speak. *I can't,* she thought. *I just can't get up in front of everyone and talk—especially* not *about my life.*

Before going to bed, Sepia prayed, "Dear God, please make me strong. I am afraid to get up in front of everyone and speak."

The following day, Sepia wrote her biography. She wrote about her family's escape from their homeland, a country where people were persecuted if they believed in God. She told how God had given her father an escape plan. After she finished her biography, Sepia prayed again: "Dear God, please make me strong. I am afraid to get up in front of everyone and speak." As she prayed, Sepia felt a peace come into her heart and she knew God would help her.

The next day she was able to share her story with confidence.

Prayer does make a difference. Just as Sepia prayed and asked God to make her strong, you too can ask God to make you strong enough to stand up against your fears and doubts.

Do you have a prayer similar to Sepia's?

_____

What is it?

_____

_____

_____

Is there anything in Ephesians 6:10–20 that you would like to pray for or do?

_____

_____

_____

Today's prayer:

_____

_____

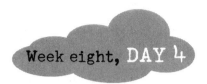

PRAYER DEFEATS SATAN

So, obey God. Stand up to the devil. He will run away from you. Come near to God, and He will come near to you. —JAMES 4:7–8A

Have you ever had to stand up to anyone? _____ What did you do or say?

_____

_____

_____

It happened again. Hunter knocked Dan's book bag on the floor, called him names, and messed with his hat. Dan didn't like riding on the school bus anymore. His assigned seat was next to Hunter, a well-known bully. Sitting next to him was not fun. One day, Dan remembered the Bible verse that said to pray for those who hurt you, so he began to pray for Hunter every day. He asked God to give him His love for Hunter and words to speak to him. One day, Dan asked Hunter what he liked to do when he wasn't in school. Hunter said that he liked to go fishing. Soon they began talking about fishing and the fishing trips they had gone on. The two boys were becoming friends, and later Dan noticed that Hunter was not bullying him anymore.

God calls us His friends and the devil our enemy. Every good gift comes from God and all evil comes from the devil.

In today's Bible verse, we are told to obey God and stand up to the devil. If we do, the devil will run away. But how do we stand up? We stand up to the devil by coming close to God through obedience and prayer as Dan did.

Where and when do you need to stand up to the devil?

_____

_____

_____

Today's prayer:

_____

_____

_____

_____

_____

_____

_____

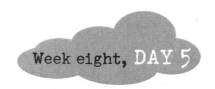

PRAYER SHAPES HISTORY

Another angel came and stood at the altar. He had a shallow gold cup for burning incense. He was given a lot of incense to offer on the golden altar in front of the throne. With the incense he offered the prayers of all God's people. The smoke of the incense together with the prayers of God's people rose up from the angel's hand. It went up in front of God. —REVELATION 8:3–4

Your prayers during the past eight weeks have risen like incense (smoke that smells good) upward to the throne room of God. He listens to you, and He loves to hear you pray. Look back through your book at what you wrote down and answer the following questions.

What special prayers have you prayed in the past weeks?

_____

_____

_____

_____

What prayers has God already answered?

_____

_____

_____

_____

_____

How has prayer made a difference in your life? In the lives of others? In your neighborhood? In your city?

_____

_____

_____

_____

_____

After you finish this book, do you think you will pray more often?

_____

How will your prayer life be different?

_____

_____

Have you found someone to pray with?

_____

If not, email Pebbles and Stones and we will pray with you: Info@pebblesandstones.com. Tell us your name and your need in the email.

Today's prayer:

_____

_____

_____

_____

_____

_____

_____

ABC METHOD*

ADMIT

ADMIT you're a sinner. Everyone has done things that displease God. No one can live perfectly. He says no sin can enter heaven. Something must be done to get rid of your sin.

Only what is pure will enter it. No one who fools others or does shameful things will enter it. Only those whose names are written in the Lamb's Book of Life will enter the city. –Revelation 21:27

BELIEVE

BELIEVE Jesus died on the cross for you. God loves you and wants you to become His child. He loves you so much that He sent His Son, Jesus, to shed His blood to save you from your sins. He took your place on the cross, and died for you. Believe that He died for you, was buried, and rose again on the third day.

Believe in the Lord Jesus Christ, and you will be saved. –Acts 16:31 NIV

ONFESS

CHOOSE TO CONFESS your sinfulness to God. Ask Jesus to save you—trust in Him as your Savior from sin.

If you confess with your mouth that Jesus is Lord and believe in your heart that God has raised Him from the dead, you will be saved.
—Romans 10:9 NIV

Everyone who calls on the name of the Lord will be saved. —Romans 10:13

If you believe in Jesus and have placed your faith and trust in Him, God has forgiven you. Then you, along with all the others who believe in Jesus, will spend eternity in heaven with Him.

*This information was taken from *Kids Love to Pray Too!* curriculum.

PRAYER OF SALVATION*

If you have never prayed to ask God to forgive your sins and for Jesus tobe your Savior, you can pray this prayer:

Father God,
I understand that I am a sinner,
And that I need a Savior.
I believe Jesus died to save me.
I believe You raised Jesus from the dead.
I accept Jesus as my Savior.
I ask You to forgive my sins and make me a new person.
I want to serve You and live for You the rest of my life.
In Jesus' name I pray, Amen.

*This information was taken from *Kids Love to Pray Too!* curriculum.